One 'n Done #12

The Heart Decided to Move

by
Melanie Bell

Published by

Read
Furiously

Read Often. Read Well.

Published by Read Furiously - Trenton, NJ. First Edition.

ISBN: 978-1-960869-19-7
Library of Congress Control Number: 2025933429

Mixed Media
Memoir
Poetry

This is a work of fiction. Names, characters, business, events and incidents are the products of the author's imagination. Any resemblance to actual persons, living or dead, or actual events is purely coincidental.

For more information on *The Heart Decided to Move* or Read Furiously, please visit readfuriously.com. For inquiries, please contact info@readfuriously.com.

Read: [*v*] The act of interpreting and understanding language, symbols, and the written word.

Furiously: [*adv*] To do something with excitement and passion.

Read Often. Read Well.
Read Furiously

To immigrants around the world.

Object
in
Motion

The Heart Decided to Move

The heart decided to move.
It packed its boxes,
swept up,
and got its deposit back.

In a new flat
stinking of fresh paint
It sets down arteries for roots.
It doesn't know
if it will be here long.
Here it is now.

It calls this place "home"
to rhyme with "roam"
which it has done
time and again
and might continue
or might not.

Ancestry Visa

"Where in the States are you from?" they ask.
"Oh, Canada, I'm so sorry!
Canadians are so nice!
But why *here?*"

A complicated question
fueled by rootlessness, a yearning to explore,
my American parents in Canada
the only ones without relatives local,
"Come from away."
A grandfather born back in Scotland
because his mother hailed from there.
Moving's in the blood.

Homeward

White girl who blended in
on Micmac land long taken from the Mi'kmaq
where fiddles sang to fiddleheads
and kids lived by Mémé and Pépé, Opa and Oma,
your parents came North to begin

digging the red ground
and went back down again every year
below Maine's mountains, family'd appear
with one story, though your mother tells another—
your people come from sheep-folds, frostbite, craggy
silver stone.

Grown again, alone
you try one passport, then another,
leaving brothers for the States,
maple leaves for sun, then rain,
crossing from one island to another,
Gaelic words familiar though you've never spoken
one.

Familiar drawl of bagpipes at the corner
selling wares for tourists even here—
kilts no one would wear,
plush woolly cows that look like bears.
Rain drums the hilltop castle bus stop.

The real thing's speech that rolls and lilts
and seats that let your short legs reach the floor.
Here chubby babies' faces look like you
(Do too many look like you?)
and your grandma's shortbread sold in tins as
hilltops close in green.
Small finds that you weren't looking for,
small truths no one can speak—
your people come from hard rain, high song, stories
left in stone.

Commute by Tube

The tube hums and beeps
"Mind the closing doors"
sounding ever so polite.
Such clear enunciation,
what must that gig pay?

Heavy press of sweaty bodies
standing, stamping, queuing,
half of them black-coated, me included,
wouldn't hurt to have some neon green in there.

A rotating cast of adverts
vie to entertain us.
"You've found your perfect match in a degree
programme.
Now find the matching owls."

They know we all want
a new job, a better office,
takeaway at meetings or at home,
that blockbuster thriller novel
that never makes it onto posters in the States.

Among it all hang panels of poetry.
Sometimes there's only an excerpt,
leaving us hanging.
We'd have to go digging
to read the whole poem.

Fear

After Ciaran Carson

I fear my life's a slowly waning rhyme
whose passage spills too quickly out of hand.
Did I say "passage?" No, my fear is time
that drifts of its own will beyond command.

I fear the wheel, the spreadsheet, and the grave
will lick me up and spit out every bone.
I fear that every bit of love I gave
will vanish, and someday I'll stand alone.

I fear the future and I fear the past,
hope-shards and dream-dust scattered on my lawn.
I fear that nothing good from me will last
but all the bad I've done will carry on.

I fear that I'm too little for my will.
I fear that my ambition looms too large.
I fear someday my family will fall ill
and leave my own incompetence in charge.

I fear I'll travel on from place to place

and—oh, my friends, this is a sorry fear—
soon no one that I know will know my face.
I fear that I'll be gone while I'm still here.

FetLife

At the Asian food court
at a queer women's meetup,
the woman two seats down from me
tells the table she's a fitness domme.

"The men pay me to lose weight.
If they don't meet their goals,
I take their money."

To the curious listener next to me
she recommends FetLife,
smiles knowingly when I say
"Yeah, I'm familiar with it."

Turns out she wrestles near my place.
"Fantasy wrestling too.
The men try to push me off the chair and I stay there."

"Is it always men?" asks the woman beside me.
"Yes," she assures.
"It's always men.
Would *you* pay to do that?"

The Fruit at Work

The fruit at work
appears on random days.
I think they bring them once a week,
plus extra times. Surprise!

Bananas go,
and tang-juiced clementines.
The pears will sometimes last awhile,
their skins half green, half brown.

Poor old apples,
those suckers hang around.
Hard, deep red orbs that no one wants,
as bland as paper bags.

We wait for fruits
and hoard them at our desks.
Like baby birds with open beaks,
we take what is given.

Desk Birthday Cake

I told no one it was my birthday.
Went to a meeting for two hours,
another for one.
When I got back,
the cake had appeared.
Tricolored remnants of someone else's party
sitting on the ledge where colleagues shared their
treats
for others to partake.
Did someone else have a birthday
people knew about?
Someone who'd worked there for more than three
months
with a boss who'd been there for two?
Did I miss a song?
I pulled off a cheap blue paper towel
and set a thin slice on top.
It tasted like the colored sweets,
Neapolitan, Bubblegum ice cream, rainbow chip,
you eat as little kids.
I told no one it was my birthday too.

Badger, Badger, Badger

Striped childhood friend,
mascot of the Hufflepuff common room,
star of a French class story
enshrining the magic of winter,
quaint as a Narnian faun
who, much like you, I've never met.

I mean to meet you eventually.
It's been three years—
do you or I procrastinate?
I've met the quick red fox five dozen times,
the rat in the subway, the mole not yet.
Now where do you hang out?

Kindly badger in your set,
will you come if the winter snows
like in that book when I was eight?
Lead me through the shadowed wood
and under magic's gate?
Badger, here I wait.

"Write About Your Perfect Day"

The shape of a perfect day slips by
like the word on the tip of your tongue,
the lyric left unsung,
the itching to act in your thumb.

Your hopes left undefined,
as vague to you as your mother's heart
or your father's wish to start anew
or the cultural narrative's urge to do—

Just what, you cannot say.
You sit and wait another day
for a letter to come in the mail
from a pen pal overseas

though the letters stopped flying fifteen years back
along with your sense of ease
and the childhood home chipped to splinters
and the breeze—was it breath?—that danced
through those trees

'til you followed them back and back.
Here's the stark white rock where you'd stand when
a lack
emerged in your stinging soul,
before you felt old, and aches bent your back

from years at a desk too high.
It was here that you looked to the sky
and here is the place you will always be
at the back of your heart, by the old spruce tree.

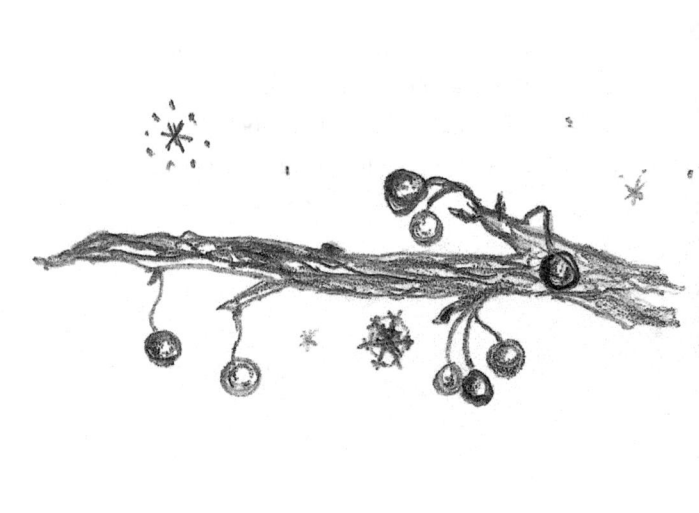

Prior
Wanderings

The Things You Shed

Knifepoint biting into boxwood,
the toy-box pungent sawdust
stirs a fury of flakes.

We waited for the fire, cedar chopped minuscule,
wedged to spark the tent of long-cut pine.
Cold-frame sweat lodge,
sage on racks of hewed branches.
We waited for the blankets,
creased in with mittened moth hands,
to blot out 9 a.m.

Languorous,
the object uncurls itself.
Ribbons of molasses lace its rounding skin.

I huddled in Irish sweater and too-thin patterned skirt,
Navajo à la Salvation Army,
a zigzagged blanket round my waist—
genuine Maliseet,
at least the giver was.
We waited

We waited
for prodded rocks to spark.

It grows a snout,
a handle still too fat,
shavings like watermelon lopped from a half-rind bowl.

Four directions round the circle,
scattering powder from a plastic can,
its drooping-cigarette slogan
Tobacco causes impotence.
Squelch feet from mud to rug,
shuck off knee socks
as cherry-glowing stones are pitchforked in.

Unspeakable, it says
and will not be touched further.
Scrapings in the plastic bag mound wider than the
spoon.

Four rounds sizzling with cedar-wafted water smoke,
enclosed in a hemisphere smelling of blueberries,
huddling with prayers.
We daub ourselves with towels

Anytime… you can come back here
anytime with the sizzle of—

                              too thin, the knot is closing.
                        Mobius-like, it will never stop
                  its meandering inward, its trellising out
                                         and back
                                         and back

anytime, unfold your ragged coat
and step in liquid-shouldered.

Howard's Cove

Crabbing toes on sandstone, Howard's Cove air smells of fish plant. Bodies processed, scales unhinged to refuse. We make a barefoot line. A stride of seven bathing suits and T-shirts. Swimming trunks and jean shorts. The beach here is all height.

Our lust's above the water where we wander cliff to cliff on this pink shoreline. Each is plugged with marram grass, eroding to a drop. Another cliff-face, can't tell one from another, sandstone plunge from neighbour. Fifty feet at least down.

Hair's all wind and blinder, salt's all water. They join hands on ledges and raise their chests and stand there. Waves are summoned leapers, whipping high as chests to drench them. Whitest T-shirts choked to amber, sounding rush of thunder. I'm not there.

Waves rain in among them. I'm off watching, standing too far, feet crabbed into marram grass, the water's rising walls. Not walls but grabs inhuman that could tear them, thrust them under. So white the dots of spray, so small, for walls that close above their heads and dark the jutting solids of their chests.

The air is a benefactor, a putrid pinch to wake from water. Reach a fissure, there's a valley to the next one. Let them clamber. Watch the nesting swallows flicker from one cliff hole to another. Watch the piping plovers peck beside the pebbled river.

Finally leave the marram grass to go there. Feel the lawn grass by the river, all is greener. Feel the stones, inhale, it's dryer. Dip in finger, taste no salt. Name what's apprehended and the apprehension falters. Just say "leaving" and the captured gaze is blinkered.

Wind brings waves too tall for dryness. From the valley, watch the others on the red heights, nest hole-riddled. Standing there above me, forts of water rising off them. Still my chest refuses any single amber drop.

Letters from Inuvik

1. Laundromat
To a friend

Our lines parallel on gravel roads, the cavernous carpet where houses will be built (someday) on Gwich'in Time—pebbles scoured by the sea, bleached the same colorless tone. In August foxtails grow there. Mornings walking past, the once-parched space is sun in every filament.

The town, laundered, has emerged in tatters, hung out on top of the world to dry, 24 nightless hours. Every step domed in close. The desiccated laundromat air. Buildings' stilts pegging ground, upside-down clothespins.

Every rainfall the grey mists greyer. Ravens plumped, swollen like raisins in water, feathers glossy, flight too swift to define their silk. Their alarm calls a child's strangled croak.

I wandered into the park one morning in your absence.

Clouds heavy, fringed with dark. Washing day and the swings gathered pools. Ground pulled my sneakers into the feel of drag.

My next time there, the sun had forgotten immortality. The sky grapefruit pink. It would not yet darken.

2. Wild Roses
To a penpal

No imprint of a saucer crowns the soil, just a ring of dust where one might have been lifted. Fingers have pressed seeds here, indenting chocolate pellets in cappuccino soil.

Shrubs are tall and conifers bonsai. Spring has spilled over with brambles in a virtueless musk. In one day the buds unravel their calligraphy: This is not like home.

Roots aren't nourished upward from the sewer— petals filigree beneath utilidors, piping graffiti the sky.

Above the scaggle of craggy stubble a yellow butterfly, a note origamied, flung into the wind.

3. Grace
To a guide

The ancestors gash fish with a half-moon ulu. *Thunk-thunk. Thunk-thunk.* One half of the circle of life is the space where it ends, your finger on the notch where it began, the rest sliced away.

White flesh. Chunk by chunk (the children boil it in the pot). The first time I've tried intestine, and nothing is ever wasted. They offer me a cut and watch me chew.

When the elders hew it open they proffer heart, lungs, clots of fat to waiting hands. The cook hates chicken breasts. No bones. (No life.)

Here bannock is birth-day cake.

The outhouse is more fragrant than expected—reeks of sewage, resin wood, coniferous air. To get there, scramble over roots. Sleep comes hardest when the campers are sound. Watch the sun stall—it's later now, suspended in a half-circle dream, until morning tugs it up again. The water, golden and wild rose, asymmetrical.

This is panoramic. Breathe a prayer for understanding. Spirits awaken in the pines.

Authenticity

Seven eagles sighted boating.
Think, the land sustains us.
Gravel on gravel on gravel
with a core of shifting ice.
Do not ask how much the groceries cost at NorthMart.
Bob the trucker brings better ones fresh from British
Columbia—
oranges from South America, crackers in packages
Made in China.

Amid stalls of dryfish and hot goose soup,
renounce vegetarianism.
Chomp hot dogs with kids at camp,
so hungry it becomes another ritual.
Never ask for seconds
but steal handfuls of marshmallow mix from
whale-coloured bowl in staff room
for a week afterwards, gnawing gelatin jerky.

Feign expertise at sorting kids in rows.
Command the unbelieving 'til voices chant in tune.
Corner-bound, listen.

Do not decipher the words.

Think shaman over mixing bowls.

Think spirit helpers in there somewhere, garbed in
furs.

Do not sing or it will be in the wrong language.

Do not think of "wanting to get out of here."

Do not think how parentless they roam.

Think callback.

Think drone, think wide sky,

something like the anthem of hands

that make a mending of reeds and wood-gnarls and
dye.

Think your skin a lie.

De retour

1.

Hips figure-eighting to the throb of salsa,
the Balzas sashay through their duplex day.
Bienvenue à Montréal:
the first day we visit la fruiterie and plump our cart
with apples to quince, a cornucopia of treeflesh I
didn't know existed.
Le quartier chinois est par-ici,
et par-là, le voisinage grec, parading flags for a soccer
triumph.
Me voici installée dans une garderie
avec les petits—Rania, Alyha, Anas—et un roman
québécois.
The Tunisians who own La Garderie speak my
French,
the kind with an accent.
En la casa, Mamie habla español.

2.

Three years. The snow mutes our bootfalls,
stifles each double-socked foot.
My toes numb anyway.

Le chemin m'échappe. Je dois te suivre.
La neige profonde fait taire notre haleine.

I catalogue familiar houses
and startle at lawns of electric reindeer where gera-
niums grew.
You coach me on my accent—my tongue
runs too light, lacks the power to grind gravel.
J'essaie de mon mieux, sans pouvoir,
sans le pouvoir de comprendre.

The house at the butt of the street is locked.
Turning downtown, the decals of a fast food restau-
rant.
We've reached the end of the road, I say,
skimming the sound tentative through our ears.
Carnivorously, we two vegetarians gnaw the sizzled
fries.
The path escapes me. I have to follow you.
The deep snow makes our breath quiet itself.

Mothernever

My mother never went to Vegas, took a plane to
where the skyline
canyoned. Never slept with the strange man who'd
been to Thailand, never
spoke with girls in black whose skin smelled of
crushed flowers.

My mother never walked the strip alone, she never
saw the smiling dolphins lightshow fountains Caesars
Palace never
caught volcano's sparking cone, heard crowd
Isscoming Shh

Issgonnasplode
before it   did

They say my mother used to be a mountain goat in
Europe now
her daughter's sitting blanketed in leaves before four
arches, thorned red branches.
Arches bring good luck she thought her mother told
her, talking about France—

her mother'd missed her chance, misread the
landmarks, fortune never
guaranteed. For years the daughter'd sanctified
McDonald's, beatified the curves
of broken trees. False idols. What luck she had she
doubted came from them.

My mother never went to Asia, took her path to oft
beaten skies, she never
sunk her head in fountains, never drowned in orchid
petals' arches never
picked zucchini fields or sang into the stables, never
loved

to whisper *Shhhhh*
                Shh

motherneverdaughter

cruised the false canals inside the hotel malls or
strolled the plastered Paris never
tried on fur designer, never stayed for free or ate for
free or rode the coaster never
slept inside a pyramid of rats or held the girlman
smelled his Thailandpetal skin.

Of the Miles

Hand out the window, grasping
for flies. Eyes
graze the dashboard,
scrying for lights.

Bass throb scatters, bay scalds
nostrils stellated with salt
in the musk rose cloud-light
ceilinged in smog. Pulse. Drift.

"Freedom!" you shriek
and lights like earthbound constellations
glance off bridge, store-rows, streets of pillbug cars
refracting, re-refracting
where they wait like cast-off locust shells.

Fortissimo pedal. "No one can know you here!"
Surge. Veer.
Lunging forward, we down the elixir
of apathetic asphalt on a hard-rock night.

Language Lessons

Kuzuzangpo-la
(Translation: Hello)

Strain eardrums over surface of this teaching room,
a hemisphere away from the hum of a language
absorbed as a kid.
   Wake up
and everyone's silked in kira and gho, body has
rocketed
itself 'cross the ocean, all sounds are complexity
circling
these words becoming third, not-English not-French,
what's French for them but my plump noise *Bon-joor*,
this circle of undergrads
standing talking Does sound have a different
quality on mountains
(Maybe we won't be here long)

  Ga de bay yoe la?
  (Translation: How are you?)

Wince at this mis/fit   numb
feet wrapped in the remnants of a grammatical
structure.
Welcome to the Language Centre
New sounds and I, slip.
Having been well fed
(—silken berry cheesecake, used book store,
intimate knowledge of construction—)
had resolved to try another climate, the words
          nonsense
although I'd felt their spaces back home, conditioned
into sentence, counted raisins
more melodious when I could remember numbers
(anticipating chili),
faces wrinkled and strange.

          Di gachi mo?
          (Translation: What is it?)

What is stranger— silly sound,
what is almost home,
hangover, university internship, cross-cultural
communication,
immunization to what?

Do I taste of invasive snow?

> *Nga choe charo inn.*
> *(Translation: We are friends.)*

We are only strangers when we're crossing
while language, missed, new, and host to my shuf-
fled-off condition,
persists dropped in with bread and leadership cours-
es and Socially Useful Productive Work
and a couple new rice cheese words per day
makes learning *namey samey* fast.
My ear culls senseless artifacts, saturation,
full if basic conversation (—when a glorious exis-
tence is possible for me,
chattering in tangible rhythms,
more trips, consumer vote—)
about a mango I am splitting to eat.

> *Choe gi ming gachi mo?*
> *(Translation: What is your name?)*

Hard to attach mnemonics to unimagined word
species

       (the hum and most
       of what I know groping, grappling.)
Knife around attempting cognates,
golden flesh to sweeten singe of *ema* (chili), *chilip*
(foreigner with infant tongue).
Am chukulay, mango, little mother?
       (the hum and most
       of what I know almost imperceptibly rounding out.)

Shell

In silk, all women are gladiolas.
I learn how to cinch the kira around my waist—
machine-woven, says Tshering.
My hands are mine, familiar spiders.
Nothing in the mirror is strange.

You're beautiful, ma'am,
the youngsters lilt their English
yards away to the calcite of my skin.

I don't notice how Dawa's face powder
is five shades too pale for her cheeks,
how everyone's flesh is glaze-immaculate, how
everyone's coiffed
with satin-black rill, singed chemically straight.

Can I call you goray? teases Yam,
unsheathing roguish teeth.
Dawa, the moon, offers me her name.

Roommates press a button on their cell phones.
Record this benign intrusion from North America

to hang on their walls when I'm gone.
Other times, three of four travelers,
rice-skinned, are enough
to restore the balance I'm used to.

Does your family have servants, Malanie?
No. Never did, and yes, I did grow up with potatoes,
cows next door, and mice in the closet. I'm not afraid of yours.

But for a moment I'm suspended on the Nokia screen,
chalk shell beached in tan-gold pebbles,
the only girl with close-chopped curls
and eyes of colonial blue.

"It is like that only"

On the porch, Yam whirls the prayer wheel. Gilded
crimson swish.
We shed our sandals on the threshold
but there is no altar in this house,
Hindu Nepal within Buddhist Bhutan.
No silken windsocks. No shelved idols with their gilded
moustaches.
No curl-edged, lotused cabinet molded to the room.
No roostered rugs, but couches shawled in knitted
neon,
tuliped chalets in Switzerland on the walls,
and a mat for the guest's comfort on the wooden floor.

Yam's sister has made shel roti.
"You pound the rice and leave it in water overnight."
At home I'd buy flour
to sculpt these doughy wreaths. Onion rings, I think,
translating. But there are no onions
and the chewing persists.
This is sacred bread.
Sharing shel roti, Roichal assures,
ensures we will meet again.

Were he a citizen,
a government post would lure his grin.

In the Hindu temple, a cottage with Christmas lights
and tacked-up paper gods,
we gather in jeans to jingle hymns of Krishna
above the hollow-reed chant of nearby monks
whose stipends have doubled.
(The same newssheet announced Nepali bombs
beneath the unveiling of a mural of the
Royal Family, cherry blossom-swathed in silk.
Yam is loyal to the King.
His uncle, less so.)

Nakay

Wombed in a temenos of concrete walls,
in the rice cooker's residual hum,
Sangay brings a curry that slivers
the toad-hide on my tongue.
Nakay, the damp curls of embryo ferns

like the splayed antennae of the junebug
that crawls up plum-sized in the first squat toilet.
In the boys' hostel a viper coiled beneath stairs—
or was it a cobra?—they spent an hour debating
while it lounged, sinuous, in wait.

Curfew close, I tell her I'm not afraid
to be alone, this where no one is ever alone
and bogeydog noises catch like nettle
and boulders lurch to cowhood on the road.

A month and the road is grooved in my hippocampus.
I've grown more venturesome, my steps less sure,
sprung with shadow flickers—leaf or limb?—
and strangers' shorn syllables overheard.
I clutch my beads in reverence to ghosts.

Om ah hung baza guru padma sidhi hung.
The dark is
nothing but the lack
of that which paints our skin,
names us ourselves.
Om ah hung baza
Om ah hung…

Larynx, the damp curl of embryo fern.
A rip of tension thrills through knotted shoulders,
runs savage in the ligaments of neck.

Spit Island

where trees grow gloriously but not too high
where constellations spill their milk at night
where you can throw a rock without hitting a
neighbor's window
water the hostas around the rotting barn as you spit

red mud bundle where peaceable people retire
and kids end up, end up again
a citizen conveyor belt
where due to a yard of flowers I turned to poetry

fall leaves sent up tiny exclamations, love so easy,
chapping winds an easy price for annual currants on
time,
those and schoolkids' favorite jeer *that's so gay*
'cause everything on this island is so damn fertile

seacoast borders everything, reeking of fish
I watched her dive, so easy not to admit
I hear the economy's failing
I hear all the kids are leaving

all I see when I return are trees and crops and things
no plays or concerts or easy entertainment say the guys
but it's worth it to have the space, find our own things to do
I couldn't take the city

maybe I'd take you there, keep you in a trailer as if that
would work
grind our deviant trails into the red dirt
elevate loneliness to virtue due to the soothing view
surrender your liberty for berries in our mouths

New World

Prodigal, sing madrigals along the mountain track.
Don't leave crumbs to mark your way back, or
anything more enduring.
Your stranger's coat, the stranger you see, are just
objects for the graphing.
Is your skin a story waiting for an ending?

Do / Don't feed the rodents (hungry, cloakless) that
can scavenge for themselves.
Eat the pie no matter what's baked inside, or dip a
finger in to test and risk offending the baker.
Eat the meals proffered on leaf plates. The answer
may or may not depend on the results of the above.
Trade cows for beans or whiskey for beaver pelts.
Name the place you land on for the place you meant
to get to, believing it's the same.

One naming will alter the span of a lake,
its consciousness a will that's slowly circling
and will a thing you've always found unnerving,
sapping nervous systems' workings, ever marching.

Will a white feline beheaded become woman or dead
kitten?
Is there something friendly zipped inside that
bearskin?
Do people living in the trees disturb you?
Do their certainties unmoor you?
Do you fear them as you fear snakes?

Find a dragon twined in your intestine.
Claws outstretched, entreating —
Sign this treaty. Clauses seal with naming all you see.
Do / Don't craft yourself a quill and write a blessing
(since your loneliness is telling).
Falsify its signing.
Accept a stranger's healing.

A promise to go back is stored in the fat of your
calves.
They grow muscled, excess drops like hail.
The trees are too thick-backed for you to ascertain a
trail.
Do / Don't stay away until your certitude is halved.

When the
World Shut
Down

Corona 2020

I lodge in your spittle
with impunity.
They say I am the punishment for your unity.
I want only to propagate myself.
Is that so bad,
to want what you all had?
You won't have it much longer now.

Amid the grass, a crocus blooms
that you won't see.
The underground trundles on,
cutting its service down.
More airplanes take to the ground.
Read books, says social media,
paint pictures,
as if your celebrations will stop me.

Take to your apartments as I have taken to the
streets.
Get delivery, stockpile TP,
metamorphose your meetings to emails,
cease your buying, buying, buying,

running, racing, being
invincible in your minds.

Unwind
your picture of the world
from the dream you believed it to be.
Blot out the charcoal portrait
you believed yourself to be.
Who are you now once rituals have gone?
What do you now want?

I only want
to be more,
to be bigger,
to spread and spread around—
the very dreams you held for yourself
and outgrew
in a room
by yourself
with the curtains drawn
in the back of your heart
when your mind is gone
where you watch the shadows of the sun.

Grace in the Time of the Virus

Take this time
for yourself.
Everyone around you
is doing the same,
snatching the last eggs from air.
You start, you care
a little too much,
don't finish the chapter
you intended to write.
Everybody's chapters
are unfinished, now,
some cut off mid-sentence,
the foot suspended midair,
the period still to come.

You are alive.
Remember, every breath,
hold in the droplets
lest they infect.
Act as if you are the virus.
It lives inside all of us now,
eating our cereal, oatmeal,

that bread we were lucky to get.
So does grace.
Remember, it whispers,
not to touch your face.
This is how best to avoid
a shelter in place.

Grace puppets your body
and motivates your limbs.
Grace closes restaurants and gyms.
Grace in the faces of loved ones on the screen,
of tweets reaching out,
all those hearts behind the news, news, news,
all those people dancing in their kitchen
and smiling at you.

In the Media, Early Days

We will work from home
for the foreseeable future
the new normal
managing families while perched
on the edge of kitchen chairs
crafting DIY teddy bears
an influx of citizens baking sourdough

Clicking the day away—
"The Disney princesses in quarantine!"
Should all these fashion brands be selling masks?
Personal trainer runs lockdown aerobics class on her
street
while standing on a portable toilet—

Now is a terrible time for productivity.
Now is a great time to write that novel.

Easter Shopping in Apocalypse Times

The lines wind halfway round the wall,
marked with security tape.
Guards in yellow vests move us onward—
two meters' distance,
single file.

The eggs are back,
a timely resurrection.
A few bags of pasta peek shyly from their shelf.
Into the basket tumble British sweets
I've never eaten before,
and—ahh—fresh kale, bunny leaves
bagged to carry home.
I ponder flowers with no vase,
wind-up chicks and rabbits,
and leave with protein bars.

Run

So tired of the blood in my ears.
Six feet away—
dodge, weave, flee.
It is suddenly polite to cross
to the other side of the street
fearing strangers' hands,
the single finger touching mine at the market stall.
Run, run, run
keeping the finger away
from face, from its fellows,
running all the way home
to rub it through with soap
and hope.

Water—my throat so tight
it's easy to forget to drink.
London is on lockdown,
stay at home, don't greet your friends
(I don't have any here,
just the work that followed me home
burrowing into the beanbag chair—
Be happy, be happy

you've still got income, though barely enough)
Police to break up groups, not fights,
a single jog, longer and longer each day.
I'd thought it would be nice to be the kind
of person who ran in the park.
Look who's running now.

Viseophones

I watched a striped bird eat a piece of bread,
observed a cat fight in which, from my window,
I could only see one cat.
The neighbors' tree blooms bounteously pink.
I wish you could see it
outside of the photos from my phone.

I wish I could talk to someone
I don't see every hour
who isn't a pixelated face.
Remember back in third grade,
how excited we were at the prospect of
"viseophones,"
imagining telephones with video screens, snapping
and bright?
They run the world now,
static crackling, sometimes crashing.
All. These. Screens.

"Look," says my brother,
pointing to the green screen flashing patterns
he's set up to replace the sweater on his chest.

"I can change my shirt!"
Colleagues toast each other—
same city, different flats,
no closer than if they sat in China.
Viseophones light up every window.

Someday

Someday, when this is all over, I'll eat:
Turtles and nougat
A thick brown sandwich with tomatoes and tomato
cream cheese
Boba tea (sooner rather than later?).
I miss going to Chinatown.
I miss having adventures.
I miss closing my eyes and pretending I was a star
as if that still mattered
now that all the stars are housebound too.

Someday I'll make rice and it'll come out just right.
Someday I'll be happy to have company,
stop wishing everyone would lay off the phone calls
and meetings onscreen.
Someday it won't be the end of the world.

Where's the Supermoon?

Google said it'd pop out in the morning
while daylight swabbed British skies.
I waited twelve hours for this apparition
until sunset tracked flamingo-pink and
damson-purple
smears across the sky
where the moon was *supposed* to show up.

Cats came and went out of the hole in the ivy
the local red fox dug.
Upstairs windows usually get the best view
but that night no stars sauntered over, only clouds,
earth's satellite maybe super but certainly shy,
hovering plump and pearly
over, like, Nebraska or somewhere.

Quarantainment

Red and yellow houseboats bob in the river.
By my internal clock, it's been forever
since our doors closed to anything
non-essential. Weekly shop. Daily walk.
Our feet know maps of the green paths
they can still carry us down.
Families sit in grass,
smoking weed, donning grubby masks,
mother holding child back as cat sniffs,
flicks tail, noses up to strangers.
Recalling headlines about housecats, dogs, and tigers
gasping for breath, worry fills me at his purr.

Queen Anne's lace explodes from every corner,
bluebells bloom and fade,
goslings and ducklings bob in parents' wake.
We bake coconut cake,
ferment a batch of kimchi,
try things only Pinterest dared last year.
What bird calls now?
Maybe by the end of this I'll know.

Together
and
Apart

The Water Babies
Amuse Themselves

I planted a water lily in the bath
to keep myself company.

Watched it bob between the atolls of my knees,
rhizomes worm beneath me.

On the third day it had children,
thumb-sized bodies tumbling out.

They filled the bathtub's crevasses with mud and
pebbles.
They went geocaching in my navel.

On television, sinister blue-pelted puppets,
the Ritz cracker crackle of static.

I couldn't budge to turn it off.
A fluid pooled in the lily's curled centre.

A glinting june bug crawled out pollen-backed,
sauntered into my chest cavity.

The children watched and cheered,
admiring the bug like confetti.

Wings unwrinkle from its body.
Clicking noises echo from me.

The children multiply like grubs, like seeds in spongy
berries.
The lily clings to my thighs, browns, droops.

The children learn the alphabet from song-honking
puppets,
furry and scurrilous. Drink it as soup.

They giggle at my clicking voice, my mud-caked
stomach,
my scum-tinged roots.

The Gift of Tongues

I asked for a relic.
        You granted me a bead
flat against the dew that crests my palm.

You murmured that Bede was a chronicler
like my avid pencil stub.
He wrote of Cædmon, a simple man,
loath to sing. Whether it was the words
or the tune that stayed on his lips,
the history books refrain to tell.

But miracles occur
(you fondle my fingertips)
when ground is white on white,
in the musty corners of aged wood
where a mouse tends her nest.

So it was with Cædmon.
In some aulde tongue of years bygone
(No one speaks it anymore
        you press against my lips)
a barnyard echo fell to grace his throat.

And so was born a language
in that shaded oral cathedral
kept silent for too long.

His voice gave birth, you exhale,
threading the bead around my neck.

> *Noli me tangere*

> *Tangere, tangere . . .*

I will fain please your song against the page.

Beast

Frost clings to my fur-shoulders.
I breathe splintered glass.
In the clearing, a ring of rosehips,
puckered sores on stems.
I sleep on pine boughs severed by my claws.
Hunters whistle and whisper
of a lurking shape.

Once home, they set their guns on the dust-grey floor.
The smell of musk on the holsters—something more
                    than sweat, more than meat.
            When I ask, their half-twitch grins inform
                it's not a woman's place to know.
                    At dusk I seal my eyes to hear.

Come into my house
and I will feed you
words of pure concept
unfurred by language.

        With my halting pace, unvelveted face, I come.
            With my crabapple toes in leather,

weathered from trails in the pines.

You came once, breathed on solitude
and it melted.
Pawpads shrivel with the snow
and even my jaw is wearing soft.

Thaw my cub-fists with your breath.
You know. You *know* I want to sink in your taboo hide,
become the rumble of the sound-board that's your
chest.

You sing in with your long-feathered head
bowed, a grouse that's been punctured by some
lupine barb
not mine. Declaiming *they're here, they're here,*
they, an anonymity of spruce trees
trudging row by row.

They call your name - a bleat of language- and you go.
They have planted themselves, forgotten
that their five-fingered paws
are creatures of the snow.
"Any good kills?"

Not for a long time.

                              I miss those bristly whiskers,
                   that throat whose membrane throbbing yields a
                                                        growl.

You left me with a name,
two even-hefted syllables
too light to wield.
At night, the gnashing of blunt incisors.

Reaping Early

Elaine:
Guinevere, she always got the good-looking ones.
I'll tell you, it makes a woman's chest clamp up to see
life parading by
and *her*, waxen hand cleaved to his
on the shores of the lake where her husband got
that sword.
Wasn't too polite of them to unruffled sacred
grounds
though it's possible she never asked their story.

                                              Guinevere:
                    His eyes are sealed, allowing hands of vine
                              to sap across my body unintruded.
                    Fingers numb outside my sleeves, exposed.

Don't ask me how it happened—
I'll be cursed if I know.
Cursed if I don't, either, I suppose.
Some say Fate lurks in the algae-mottled lee of the
lake.

Others reckon it's a giant squid.
But sure as dawn batters slabs of tower walls,
casting a sundial in the room where I sleep alone,
it was no squid that shut me here,
chucked a weaving loom beside me
and bid me to do as I will.

        Hurl praise at him formulaic, giggle rote.
Water rises and we clasp each other as if sap were left.
      In a few hundred years they'll invent stop signs.

The commands of its will are my secret:
there are none.
Only, when I knock against the windows,
a sting runs through my scalp.

    Fingers stutter. Legs point one way, then the next.
  Orpheus would have lived, had his heart been mute.
      Neither he nor I would have looked back.

I weave the world in clumps, because
there's nothing else to do.
The view from here slices crisper,
though I miss the proximity of song.

In the strains that carry up-forest, her voice melts to his.
I can no longer distinguish
his low notes ring flat,
her highs, sharp.

There's singing from the tower sometimes, too.
In dreams I'm looking down on fields of barley,
throat full of the keen air that means *alone*.

Sex Education

The boy, misplaced,
a top that spun counterclockwise,
named himself sharpened pen.
Ten years old he'd google innuendo,
with chin-tilt grin pronounce himself
upstanding and cocksure.

At 16 he was a virgin
who catalogued the parts—
breasts like ripe peaches haloed in fuzz,
an eyebrow curled akimbo,
the angle of an elbow
jutting out.

Later he turned to men.
He loved them for their muscles
if nothing else.
Sought in chests' taut firmness
the beached siren.
In his dreams
she had only one eye,
its clarity compensating
for the shadowed pit.

Next came promiscuity,
collisions of mutual miscomprehension.
No organs chafed him
to his satisfaction.
Was there some place,
some monastery beyond pornography?
He would burn photographs for heat,
observe the inward crinkle of outspread thighs
and all would be space,
his innards jangled and siphoned
through the titillating walls.

Elysia Erotica

One grinds thong to pole.
Another watches, palm-held drink
the gold of a juiced apple, bubbles in gullet.
In dilute light veins lace each epidermis,
here half-opalescent, here blue-mottled hide.
Another's pupils dilate towards target.

Elysia chlorotica, sea slug leaf-formed with curled
wings,
internalizes chlorophyll from algae.
Sups it up. Integrates.
Takes sunlight, makes it green
with genes from algae's atrium, pirated, locked in.
Fresh feeding organs pass into a newborn
generation.

After the lights One loiters at Another's table,
uncurls a fist, blinks, lingers.
Fingers switch a practiced arc. What kind's
the drink, they ask, indifferent to the answer.
Question an exotic dancer hides. A touch that means
something

askance from cash. Velocity of air on undersides.

Elysia's the first time genes have mixed naturally
across such a gaping gulf, come to rest
in another's cells wholesale. Plunder?
Gift, ungrudged if ungiven? After one meal,
elysia never has to eat. It simply sunbathes while
light siphons
in from sky. This is enough to place it in another
kingdom.

Yes the only answer, a word
so cliche its nucleus isn't heard. Take
and seal the verbs when the night is down,
ensconced them—not for mourning this,
not for toppling in daylight like bowling pins. Let
them be skin-thin
suncatchers. Go out rhyming: quake, awake.

In the Den

Cedar chest imprinted with molasses-flowing flame,
small hearts bordering a checkerboard,
spindle-legged ravens.
Homes with odd-numbered windows
row
by row
by row.

The cocoa you make comes bitter.
Is this how it tastes
in rain-groves
where papayas are born?

The switch on that panel where sockets suckle
phosphoresces electric.
On carpet, listing in front, five points
overturned, a crocheted anemone.

One detail—
poised on the chest—
eluded me.
This single hair-clasp,

nautical curls coppering the iris of the room,
inscrolls a universe.

Your spoon in my clasp sifts the cocoa,
milky swirls and elegiac curls
the bitterness of north star.

You Had an Eye for Glitter,

1.
A scrap of foxfire cut in your iris.
I never saw

your tacklebox laugh, the crease in your grin,
the spots of salt catching in eyelash nets. Two
species,

we surveyed each other one eye at a time
but your marble hooked my jaw.

When finally my gaze tried to sear you,
you sat. Ate something with ginger in it.
Regarded the couch.

2.
It's fun isn't it, to be alone in kitchen on new
linoleum
downing granola from a plastic bag.

To put on a plumed skirt and pretend to glide only
no one's around to see if I'm really doing it so I
could be caught mid-rapture

in levitation for all anyone'd know and the pigeons
wouldn't even give a coo. Ditch the Degas.

Come visit sometime, you and I will lap frying-pan
curries and don't dare complain
about my (most considered lack of) furniture.
Call me a minimalist.

3.
In two dimensions neither of us are photogenic.
Faces like paint chips from Colour-Your-World.
Features squashed to cheap.

Cram photos in drawer with coins, frayed ribbons,
music box with knob snapped, keys for nothing,
Q-tips, dildo.

Some apart day sequins will trail me like puppies,
follow in the bath.

I'll drink lime and see if veins run white. Grab some
stellations and see if the plastic peels.
See if the planets orbit away.

You, the Shadow You Cast

The drum in your stomach hollows
you. A waiting,
resonant in muscles loosened.
You're sundered to the floor,
rippled sheets crenellating legs just shaved,
stripped like a gourd
of its seeds

and they're looking.
Maskless bland-curious
child through the first snow's window,
itching to tumble the canvas
into angels.

There's a woman who trailed you across the wall.
You shift, and I will follow every step.
She curls in, thigh on thigh,
breast shelved on skinned-in ribcage,
breath on candle breath
but lens in focus
there's only you,
the infrared vessels that

labyrinth the space of your chest.

There's a woman in the sofa chair beside you
and later the image—
Grecian hipline bruise-butterflied,
back braced to you,
acute-angle elbow jutting to window.
Untouchable she says, *enticing*
and you're querying the real.

There are women that two parchment palms can
touch.

In Which Much Has Changed

As our faces' ridges and curves align you eye me in
the distant way one regards mountains,
intent on calculation as if that were possession,
luminous with wonder as if that were protection,
irises narrowed and alpine blue as mosaic, as marble,
as various sea and sky weathers by day.

I forget you're astonishing
when bumbling through rows of carts in Costco,
intent on lists,
knee to knee under blankets while a laptop blinks
speaking faces up at us,
when analyzing each other's least reactions.
We've curled into each other's inner space,
grateful, through terror, for each other's touch and
voice, too tired to constantly wonder.
Though my idle fancies flap to other corners now that
your coveted body nudges beside me,
little's as blessed as the presence that allows me to
forget

and to be reminded as swiftly with a handhold.

Locked toward me, your eyes hiss,
a new creature behind them, spitting blue inner flame,
arms brisk,
you lurch to tree size. I, too, from my writing desk,
can be seized with sudden lightning when your neck
bends and wheat-field hair falls down.

Once, in the absence of electric lights, we see newly,
your eyes wide and awe-frightened, mine likewise,
clutching like children, as sudden as want
we speak truths we couldn't voice with bulb-light
scorching our faces,
truths that would normally shame us
and send us out, curled together, past the corners of
an invisibly plain-white ceiling.
Time scatters like mosaic tiles or marbles.

Solid Things

Concentric circles of orange peel
dry on the ribs of a rack
beside the parsley,
white edges crimping
as aroma feathers out.

My mother crafted wreaths,
tucking baby's breath between the flames of
starflowers,
settling Spanish moss to form a base.
Her calloused fingers rooted for gold thread in cold
clods of earth.
Her needle, navigating swaths of calico,
stitched and stuffed heavy-lidded sheep,
bagged them in the attic
once, on the store benches,
they had collected too much dust.

In the mudroom corner
she hung the old sharpener
soon transmuted to a hook for brothers' coats.
The casing tumbled off.

She'd place it back over the gears,
coaching us to do the same.

I watched the iron skeleton
gnaw pencils to a point.
No one gathered the shavings
that ribboned on the floor.

Pressing a hand
to the half-moon of my shoulder,
she warned me—
look to solid things.

Serpentine cycles of orange peel
dry on the ribs of a rack
beside the parsley.
White edges crusting
as aroma withers out.

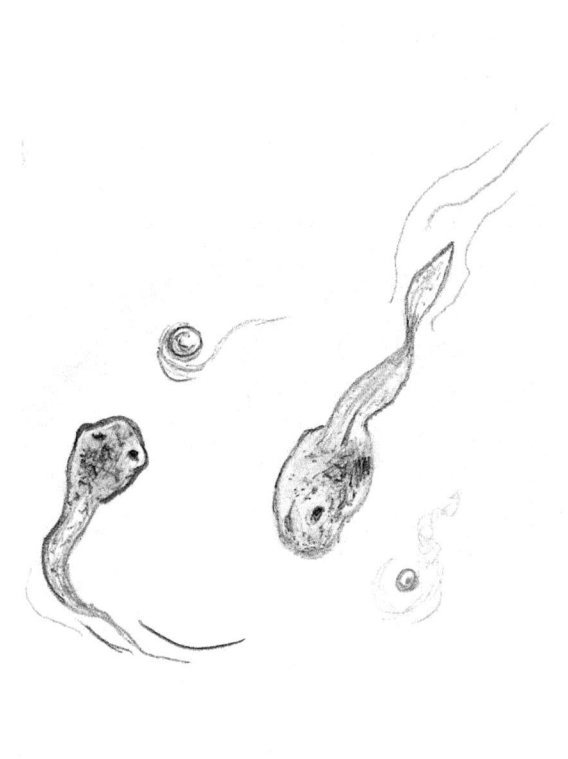

Love
After
Love

Hiking in a Group

Like riding a bike
is something I have tried
quite hard
to like.

Wouldn't it be nice
to climb that hill
and gaze upon the view?
It only takes a half a day—
or two.

Trek with strangers,
mind the dangers
of excess sun
and earnest talk
of how much fun
they had on their last walk.

Wouldn't it be grand
to understand
your temporary companions
and not to find them bland?

To catch a high
as you progress beneath the sky?

You're here. It's done.
To say that it was fun
would be a lie.

Mountain Trails

Welsh sheep trail longer tails
trotting mountainwise, fluffed with red paint
to mark whose they are.
Nothing marks me as being yours,
the lines of years light on my face,
nippy wind bracing my teeth.

This is our second railway.
We stop for an hour in the downpour,
snapping photos of soggy red leaves.
I've waited so long to move my tush
and get here.
Train whistle jolts me into worry
but it's only the engine backing up,
not our time, yet, to leave.

Directions to the Underworld

Seek a mud-thing, puddle-murky,
with eyes that look over, not into.
Who unnames shame,

who croaks desire. Follow
like a shadow,
pick the blooms and grasses from the meadow.

In one tale, go down kicking.
In another, storm down
like Ulysses, own it.

Further down than stars dive.
Further than moles,
brunt shovel to shoulder to soil.

Seek the ruler who rots like humus,
essence seen past.
Look over without looking into.

Shades sway, hands on knees,
huddled tight and quaking.

Ascertain their muttering:

We used to be glorious, didn't we?
Don't, don't you remember,
or was it only me?

Decay an apex.
Stay too long and you become hole-riddled.
Stay too long and when you rise the light goes
through you.

After the Breakup

I make French toast.
Fresh bakery slices absorb the syrup
like perfect little sponges.
Maybe the kind of love that matters
is the kind that endures,
beyond desires and ambitions—

I hold two thoughts at once:
I love you
and
This "us" was a mistake.
If it hadn't been for this dance
in whose steps we faltered and failed,
I wouldn't be here in this kitchen,
sunlight strong on my secondhand table,
enjoying this bite of French toast.

Doing My Best

"I'm doing my best," she says
as she scrolls through social media
where someone's giving a speech to the UN
and someone else's book is on a best-of list
and someone baked dozens of Christmas cookies
and someone else has a cute freaking kitten.

She pulls out a grey hair
and squeezes into jeans that used to fit better—
tighter than hoped, just like her bank balance.
Those apps are treasure boxes
where we put all our goodies.
Little more.

And what if she wasn't
doing her best?
What if she wasn't doing?
Would she still be OK?
Would she still be good
at all?

Novel-Writing Seagulls

We're crying out in the only way we know:
NaNoWriMo, 50,000 words,
the beginning of something poetic or absurd.
Stretching our inner voices every year.
meeting online thrice a week,
sharing GIFs and virtual blankets,
challenging each other to word wars.

A writer works alone, some think.
Alone with others is best.
Otherwise, how can you test yourself?
How can you stretch your limits,
and why would you
dare to climb further than you've been
without eyes to witness you or hands to catch and
guide?

We are the novel-writing seagulls.
We bark our fears into form.
Here in the city of beaches,
online, at our keyboards,
we conjure up the waves.

Shoreline Hunger

Sun-dappled snowbeasts lash ashore,
frothed with whipped cream or frosting.
Above the seagulls' raucous debates
they carve a sound larger than all of us,
a force that is greater than all of us,
that'll linger once we've died—

Not "passed away"
as waves pass to and fro
every moment of every day,
but gone. Our molecules scattered. Moved on.

I record this collage of moments
as a small child watches with sheer attention,
mind cupping to hold it all—
are they her first waves?

She waves goodbye to the spray at play,
readying itself to swallow the shoreline
that persists in existing and extending
as our lives go on.

Art Open Houses

"You could kill someone with that bracelet,"
the hostess croons at one art open house.
I grin—jagged resin rocks surround my wrist—
and think, *Perhaps I could.*
Say, instead, "I got it at another open house."

Ceramic artichokes, bulbous, cat-sized,
share space with glassy lobsters
that look good enough to eat.
Into my bag go snake-head coasters
and hearts wrapped in barbed wire.
(Last week it was bluebirds.
I'm angrier now.)

In the sculpture garden—
from house to house they blend together,
fountains flowers, things on sticks for sale—
I join the group with tea and cake,
sunshine soaking skin,
the world compressed
to sweet crumbs under my tongue.

Tadpole Time

Inky commas wiggle,
nibble algae,
new legs twitch near tails.

Above, dragonflies'
electric blue dashes
punctuate the pond.

Sinuous newts
stack overtop each other,
bend, then unbend.

Four weeks since I found them
in the park's tiny pool,
the tadpoles now sport spots.

Not a bad turnout
for this grotty ring o' water, beslimed
and overlooked in the rose garden.

Objectives

This place is too loud—
all chaos, noise, and sound.
Words string together and ring round my mind
'til sense is lost in din.

We're meant to speak up but not interrupt,
so I wait for a turn that never comes up.
Noisy roomful of patterned shirts and gowns
donned by folks whose names have gone to fog.

Presentations, declarations,
stacked-up goals and metrics—
frenetic kittens, all of us,
chasing a string around.

Nothing could be louder
than the silence that cradles failure,
the certainty of standing
on sand that should be ground.

"Have another drink!"
I think I will.
We've got too little left to lose
and just enough time to kill.

Dieppe Solitude

A grim grey beach of largish stone—
what a place to be alone.
The castle on the white cliff hill,
in this bracing wind, stands still.

In this height (without much heat)
of muggy mussel summer,
all is silent but the gulls
and a sharp, strident noise that surprises—

barks of two compact dogs,
70% louder here
as the shops boast 70% off.
On Bastille Day, fireworks go off.

A last burst of sun strikes surf,
high cream ruffles
for me, the gulls, and just a few
breathing on this beach, solemnly waiting.

The beach library's got comics for free.
A Canada garden marks history—
916 soldiers killed in the raid
in this most peaceful spot to be afraid.

Stray Feelings

Madness makes a circle.
Sadness forms a ring.
Gladness flies around
like dandelion down
and seldom settles
on anything.

Sadness plants and waters seeds
and waits for them to grow.
Madness scatters weeds
and zigzags through each row.
Gladness wanders
in search of someplace to go.

Madness hides
in tales and lies.
Sadness falls and dies.
Gladness scatters
until it finds your eyes.

Matching Up

We're many, alike in our differences,
coffee spilling on carpet,
spreading stain,
thinking our way around the world
story to story,
foreign words native on our tongues.

Not everyone sees what I now perceive
because not everyone looks.
It takes patience to know someone,
rounds at the pub or rounds of games,
unfolding layers of others over time.

Patience to trust in persistence
through the terror-joy of being known.
They pull out a chair and I sit,
having never expected this spot,
breathing shallow, hands alight with tiny fireworks,
grateful that this, too, is love.

The following poems were previously published in

"Land, Love, and My People," School of Shine
"FetLife," *Spoon Knife 6: Rest Stop*
"Howard's Cove," *Grain*
"Letters from Inuvik," *Grain*
"Authenticity," *CV2*
"V," *What We Talk About When We Talk About It*
"De retour," *The Island Review*
"Mothernever," *Sparkle & Blink* / Quiet Lightning reading series
"Shell" and "Nakay," *The Fiddlehead*
"Spit Island," *Argot Magazine*
"New World," *Cicada*
"Grace in the Time of the Virus," *Writers Resist*
"Walks in Montreal," excerpted from "Four Walks in Montreal" in *Queer Around the World*
"The Water Babies Amuse Themselves," *Silver Blade*
"Beast," *Branch* and *The Quilliad*
"Reaping Early," *Songs of Eretz*
"Inhalation" and "In Her Lesion," *Headlight Anthology*
"You Had an Eye for Glitter," *Branch*
"You, the Shadow You Cast," *Lift Every Voice*
"In Which Much Has Changed" and "Solid Things," *QWERTY*
"Directions to the Underworld," *Augur*
"Objectives," *Mensa World Journal*

Thank you to the many people who have contributed to this book: faculty at the University of New Brunswick and Concordia University; the editors of the publications where many of these pieces first appeared; and to Adam, Samantha, and the wonderful team at Read Furiously.

Thanks to my writing workshop colleagues and friends; to Kacie, my fellow adventurer; and to my family, immediate (Mom, Dad, Scott, Caleb) and extended, including the ancestors who gave me the opportunities to experience so many parts of the world.

About the Author

Melanie Bell is a Canadian multi-genre writer living in the UK. Her books include a short story collection, *Dream Signs*, a nonfiction title, *The Modern Enneagram*, the YA novel *Chasing Harmony*, and *The Heart Decided to Move*. She has written for several publications including *Contrary*, *Cicada*, *The Fiddlehead*, and *Huffington Post*. She has also written plays and a radio drama that have been performed in the UK. She loves music, art, and nature, and aspires to see as much of the world as she can.

A Note to our Furious Readers

From all of us at Read Furiously, we hope you enjoyed our latest installment in our One 'n Done series, *The Heart Decided to Move*.

There are countless narratives in this world and we would like to share as many of them as possible with our Furious Readers.

It is with this in mind that we pledge to donate a portion of these book sales to causes that are special to Read Furiously. These causes are chosen with the intent to better the lives of others who are struggling to tell their own stories.

Reading is more than a passive activity – it is the opportunity to play an active role within our world. The causes we support are culturally and socially conscious to encourage a sense of civic responsibility associated with the act of reading. Each cause has been researched thoroughly, discussed openly, and voted upon carefully by our team of Read Furiously editors.

To find out more about who, what, why, and where Read Furiously lends its support, please visit our website at readfuriously.com/our-causes

Happy reading and giving, Furious Readers!

Read Often, Read Well, Read Furiously!

More in the One 'n Done Series

What About Tuesday
Adam Wilson
978-0-9965227-9-3

Gurls, They'll Never Take Us Alive
Matt Lydon
978-1-7337360-3-9

Brethren Hollow
Bill Hemmig
978-1-7337360-8-4

Helium
Adam Wilson
and Jeff Chin
978-1-7337360-5-3

The Legend of Dave Bradley
S Atzeni
978-1-7371758-8-9

The Path Home
A.J. Pelligrino
979-8-9868097-8-6

Showboi: Too Deep Too Care
Jimmy Cullen
979-8-9868097-6-2

Wund to Space
Rowan Kilduf
978-1-960869-06-7

W(h)ine & Cheese
S. Atzeni
978-1-960869-12-8

Brooklyn Family Album
Margaret Montet
978-1-960869-11-1

Tales from the Scrapyard
Nicole Zamlout
978-1-960869-18-0

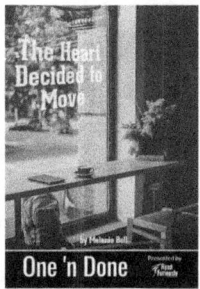

The Heart Decided to Move
Melanie Bell
978-1-960869-19-7

Small Books. Big Impact.
readfuriously.com/one

www.ingramcontent.com/pod-product-compliance
Lightning Source LLC
Chambersburg PA
CBHW071521120626
46550CB00006B/2313